Jan. 24, 2006

Responsibility

by Isaac Seder

RAINTREE
STECK-VAUGHN
RSVP PUBLISHERS

A Harcourt Company

Austin New
www.raintreesteck\

Published by Raintree Steck-Vaughn Publishers, an imprint of Steck-Vaughn Company.

Library of Congress Cataloging-in-Publication Data is available upon request.

ISBN: 0-7398-5781-9

Printed and bound in China
1 2 3 4 5 6 7 8 9 10   05 04 03 02

A Creative Media Applications, Inc. Production

Photo Credits:
AP/Wide World Photographs: Cover
AP/Wide World Photographs: Pages 5, 7, 8, 10, 11, 17, 18, 20, 23, 24, 25, 28, 29
©Students Against Violence Everywhere (SAVE): Page 22

Editor: Matt Levine
Indexer: Joan Verniero
Design and Production: Alan Barnett, Inc.
Photo Research: Yvette Reyes

Contents

"The most worthwhile endeavor I have ever undertaken is responsibility for my own life."

—LeVar Burton, actor, star of *Roots* and *Star Trek: The Next Generation*

Tell your teacher if a test tube breaks. It is the responsible thing to do.

In lab, your science teacher finds a broken test tube. The teacher turns to the class and asks, "Who's responsible for this?"

Later the same day, your English teacher finds an anonymous poem posted on the board. The poem is beautiful. The teacher reads it aloud and then asks, "Who's responsible for this?"

Responsibility can be many different things. You can be responsible for an accident, like breaking a test tube. You can also be responsible for a work of art, like a poem.

Responsibility means accepting your duties and being in control of your choices. Part of being responsible is taking care of your **obligations,** which are the things that you have to do. However, responsibility is more than doing your chores and other tasks. It is handling all of your choices and accepting the results.

This book will help you learn ways to make smart and responsible choices. It will show you how being responsible can help you take control of your life. The next time that someone asks you, "Who's responsible?" you can answer proudly, "I am!"

Fourth-grade teacher Monica McCleary leads her students in a discussion on the parts of a poem at the Hawthorne Avenue School.

Nadine agrees to baby-sit for Aunt Carol on Saturday night. Then on Friday Nadine's best friend invites her to a slumber party for Saturday. Nadine really wants to go. Her best friend is usually not allowed to have sleepovers. What should Nadine do?

The responsible choice is to stick with her original plan. No matter how tempting the party is, Nadine has a responsibility. She has told her aunt that she will baby-sit, and she should be true to her word.

Nadine decides to baby-sit and has a great time with

Is That Clear?

When you agree to do something, make sure that you are clear.

- Say what you plan to do.
- Give details, such as how and when you will complete this responsibility.
- Pay attention.
- Ask the other person to say what he or she expects of you. Correct anything that you think is wrong.

This Norman Rockwell painting, **The Babysitter,** *shows that baby-sitting is a hard job. Nadine does the responsible thing by baby-sitting for her cousins and not going to the party.*

her cousins. She knows that she will be invited to other sleepovers. When Aunt Carol returns home, she thanks Nadine for being so **reliable.**

If you are reliable, it means that people can count on you. You do what you say you will do. When people know that you are reliable, they trust you. Your responsible behavior earns their respect and appreciation.

If you do not do something that you say you will do, the job does not get done. Then you can get a **reputation** as someone who is unreliable. Your reputation is the way that people see you. It is what they think of your character. Once people make up their minds about you, it can be very hard to change them. It is much better to stick to your word.

Kyle signs up to be the editor of his school newspaper. He has fun putting together the first issue. Now the second issue is almost due. None of the articles are finished. Kyle is losing interest in the news. He is thinking about quitting.

Quitting often sounds like the easy way out of a tough situation. However, quitting does not help you meet your

Daniel Victor is editor of **The Lions' Digest,** *the student newspaper at State College Area High School in Boalsburg, Pennsylvania. With so many things to report, getting the paper out is a tough job.*

Following a Dream

Erik Weihenmayer of Colorado was born with an eye disease. By the time he turned 14, Erik was totally blind. He became very angry. He did not want others to call him "the blind kid." Things changed for Erik when he learned to rock climb. He loved the chance to use his athletic skills. Erik figured out how to make the most of his other senses to help him climb. This took hard work and perseverance. Climbing became Erik's passion. Now his goal is to climb the seven tallest peaks in the world. He reached the top of one of these peaks, Mount Everest, on May 25, 2001. Erik's perseverance helped him accomplish part of his goal.

responsibilities. A responsible student stays with a job, even when it gets tough.

Perseverance is sticking with a responsibility or task, no matter what. Whether a job is difficult or just dull, it is still your responsibility to complete it.

Of course there are many ways that you can improve a tough situation. Kyle thinks about why he is getting frustrated with the newspaper. He realizes that he is trying to do too much. He then talks to some friends about joining his team on the paper. With four other students working, the paper is once again a fun and successful project.

Patience is another key part of being responsible. You need to be patient as you stick to your duties and complete your tasks. Remind yourself that everything takes time. Do not expect everything to happen *right now*.

If you sign up for skiing lessons, you will not be zooming down the slopes on your first day. If you stick

Beginners ski on the reopened ski center on Mount Igman, in Sarajevo. This was one of the sites for the 1984 Winter Olympics.

Saving money for the future in a bank account is a responsible thing to do.

with your lessons, soon you will develop the skills that you need. A responsible beginner at any task knows that it takes time to learn something new. Your patience will pay off, and you will develop the skills that you need.

Some tasks may challenge you in new ways. Juanita is saving money from her after-school job. She is placing half of the money that she earns in a bank account. She plans to use this money for college. There are plenty of things that she could use the money for right now. However, she knows that she will need the money for college.

Self-control, or staying in charge of your emotions and actions, can help you be patient and act responsibly. Juanita shows her patience by having the self-control to save her money. If she spent it now, she would not have it for college later on. She makes the responsible decision to wait.

Jonathan borrows his best friend Tony's bicycle. While riding down a dirt trail, he falls. One spoke from the front wheel gets slightly bent. It is very hard to notice and does not seem to change the way the bike rides. Should Jonathan mention the accident? The responsible choice is to tell Tony what happened, even if the bent spoke does not make any difference.

Jonathan does tell Tony. They agree to take the bike to a shop together. The mechanic says that a bent spoke can be dangerous. Replacing it is not expensive. Jonathan pays for the repair.

Being **accountable** means accepting responsibility for your actions and their results. It is usually pretty easy to be accountable for your actions when they are positive. Taking responsibility for winning an award is not hard at all.

It can be harder to take responsibility for your mistakes. Remember that everyone makes mistakes. People are much more willing to forgive others who admit their mistakes honestly. Never try to pass the blame

Jonathan is accountable for the repair to Tony's bike.
He acts responsibly by helping Tony take the bike to a repairman.

along to someone else. Think about how you would feel if someone tried to do the same thing to you.

By acting responsibly, Jonathan turns a bike accident into an opportunity. He strengthens his friendship and his reputation when he admits what has happened.

Responsibility in the Family

Everyone pitches in on laundry day.

You might think of a family as a team. Every member of your family has special duties and responsibilities. Your family team succeeds when everyone finishes his or her responsibilities.

Some family responsibilities are simple chores, like doing the laundry or mowing the lawn. Your family might make rules for completing these chores. It is your responsibility to finish everything on time and completely. Rushing through your chores may either make more work for someone else or leave the job half-done. Allow yourself time to do your chores well.

Many family responsibilities are shared. You might share a chore like washing the dishes. Talk over your responsibilities to find a fair way to share your duties. You might decide to wash the dishes every other night. You might switch between washing and drying. Make sure that everyone agrees to the plan, and then stick to it.

Other family responsibilities include obeying your parents. When you follow their rules, your parents will trust and respect you. As you prove that you are reliable, your parents will give you more and more adult responsibilities. Remember, you earn these responsibilities by proving that you are **trustworthy.** You need to show that you can make smart choices and accept the results.

Some family responsibilities, like washing the car, are actually fun.

How to Be a Responsible Friend

Nelson knows that his best friend Luis is better in math than he is. He asks Luis to do some math homework for him. Luis wants to be a good friend, so he agrees.

Is this a responsible friendship? Are Luis and Nelson both acting responsibly?

Friends should try to support each other, but they should not do each other's work. Nelson will not get any better in math if he does not do his homework. He is taking advantage of Luis's friendship to get out of a responsibility. As for Luis, he feels like he is being a good

Friendship Boosters

Here are a few strategies that can help strengthen a friendship.

- Take a first-aid class together. You will be able to help each other in case of emergencies.
- Learn a new sport or skill together. You can help each other practice.
- Volunteer together. You might find opportunities at a local hospital, senior center, or public park.

These friends from Brownsburg Junior High School seal up boxes of donated food while volunteering at Gleaners Food Bank in Indianapolis, Indiana. Their classmates sort out arriving canned goods.

friend, but he is actually hurting Nelson.

There are better solutions. The two friends can work together so that Nelson learns his math. With this plan, both friends are also working together to build a strong, responsible friendship.

Responsible friends are honest, reliable, and **loyal,** or faithful, to each other. However, loyalty does not erase your sense of responsibility. When Marcy sees a friend take something from a store, she knows that it is wrong. She talks to her friend and makes it clear that she disapproves. Marcy's actions show that she is a loyal and responsible friend.

Sean Williamson, 11, shows responsible pet care. He offers his dog, Buddy, a drink of water at the Henderson County Fair in Stronghurst, Illinois.

Owning a pet is a big responsibility. As a pet owner, you are responsible for a living thing. Before you get a pet, you need to make sure that you have the time, money, and energy to make such a big **commitment.** You need to be 100 percent committed to owning a pet before you get one. Commitment is a big part of pet ownership, because you are responsible for the pet's entire lifetime.

Will you be a responsible pet owner? Ask yourself these questions. Answer all of them before you make your final decision.

- How much time will you be able to spend with your pet each day?
- Do you know what your pet will eat?

- Can you afford your pet's foods and toys?

- Where will your pet live? Do you have enough space?

- Does your pet need exercise? If so, how will you make sure that it gets enough?

- Does your pet need to be groomed? If so, how much time will it take?

- How often will your pet need a checkup?

- Will your pet have any special needs? How will you meet them?

Perhaps you already have a pet. If so, think about how well you and your family meet the responsibilities of owning that pet.

Think Twice Before You Go Exotic

Some pet stores sell some pretty strange animals, like tarantulas and poisonous snakes. These pets are said to be exotic, which means that they are unusual. Many people buy these pets without knowing very much about them. Most exotic pets have very special needs. Some of them do not actually make very good pets and may die in your home. It is not responsible to get a pet just because it looks weird or cool. Find out as much as you can if you are thinking of getting a pet and make a responsible decision.

Responsibility at School

You already know some of the responsibilities that you have as a student. You are responsible for getting to class on time. You have homework to complete.

Other student responsibilities are just as important. Think about your responsibilities during class discussions. You are responsible for speaking up. The more involved you are, the more you can add to the group. Sharing your thoughts is an important part of your responsibilities at school.

Responsible students work together to tackle tough problems.

These lucky students are working outside during a beautiful day. Reading and sharing ideas is one way to act responsibly at school.

What about your responsibility to act as a role model for younger students at your school? If you act responsibly and fairly, you teach younger students a valuable lesson.

Another serious responsibility you have is to help solve problems at school. Do not wait for other people to find answers. When something goes wrong, remember the saying, "If you're not part of the solution, you're part of the problem." Do your best to help out.

The students at West Charlotte High School in Charlotte, North Carolina, wanted to take responsibility for a school problem. When their classmate, Alex Orange, was shot while trying to break up a fight, they knew that they wanted to stop violence. They founded Students Against Violence Everywhere (SAVE), a group of students committed to stopping violence in and out of schools.

Bernice A. King, youngest daughter of the late Dr. Martin Luther King Jr., speaks to nearly 1,000 students at the sixth annual Students Against Violence Everywhere (SAVE) summit at North Carolina State University in Raleigh, N.C.

Role-playing helps students think responsibly about their actions.

Since it was founded in 1989, SAVE has become a leading student organization in the fight against violence. Student members learn about ways to control **conflicts,** or disagreements, before the conflicts become violent. Then they help other students take responsibility to stop violence in their own schools. Students from SAVE share their knowledge with other students in discussion groups and other programs.

In one program, two SAVE students visited another high school and started a loud fight. The fight was fake, but the other students did not know that. This strategy got students to think about how to handle the situation responsibly.

Roba Ghanayem is an officer in the SAVE club at Northern High School in Durham, North Carolina. She sees real results from her work with SAVE. "I'm finding, at least, that a lot of students are learning how to deal with their emotions," she says. She has noticed that small arguments do not seem to get out of control as much as they once did.

You have learned about responsibilities to yourself, your friends, your family, and your school. What about your responsibilities as a citizen of your town and country?

Every citizen is responsible for following laws. Many laws protect you. Knowing and following laws can help you and others stay safe.

You also have a responsibility within your community. Look for ways that you can make it safer, healthier, or just more fun. Helping out in a community garden creates beauty that everyone can enjoy. Volunteering at a senior center can help you meet new and interesting people.

A responsible citizen can also solve problems. If you disagree with something, take positive steps to correct it. For instance, Connie is unhappy when she finds that her

This stream has a flow of foamy white waste. Good citizens have a responsibility to help solve environmental problems such as this.

A Heroic Responsibility

When Nelson Mandela was a young man, South Africa followed a very unfair system called apartheid. Black citizens were forced to live in separate areas from white citizens. They did not have equal rights. Mandela knew that this system was not fair. He took responsibility for trying to change it. He spent many years fighting to create a just South Africa. He went to prison as a result of his beliefs. While he was in prison, other people continued the fight against apartheid. At last, Mandela was released and apartheid ended. When the people of South Africa were finally allowed to vote, they elected Mandela as their first president.

local stream is polluted. She learns that the source of the dirty water is a factory two towns away. Connie acts responsibly. She convinces other community members to write letters to the factory. In the letters, they ask the company to stop dumping waste into the stream.

Finally, when you are older, it is your responsibility to vote in local and national elections. It is every citizen's responsibility to make his or her voice heard. The best way to do this is by voting in every election.

Balancing Your Responsibilities

You have a lot of responsibilities. In just a single day, you might need to clean up at home, read a book for school, and write a thank-you note to your aunt. How can you make sure that you have enough time to finish all of your responsibilities?

Using a calendar is a great way to keep track of your responsibilities. Write down important dates and deadlines, and check your calendar often.

A diary or journal can help, too. Write down what you are going to do and when you are going to do it. If you tell your friend that you will bring a book to school, make a note in your journal. Check your journal every day.

It is important to balance your responsibilities. Keep track of everything that you have to do.

Decision-Making Made Easy

These steps can help you make responsible choices.

- Clearly state what needs to be decided.
- List your choices.
- List the good points and bad points of each choice.
- Discuss your choices.
- Make your choice, and follow it through.
- After a while, check your choice. Did you make the best decision? How can you learn from it?

The real key to balancing your responsibilities is to only do as much as you can. Before you say yes to something, take the time to think about it. Ask yourself a few important questions.

- Do I have the time to take on this new responsibility?
- Can I do a good job?
- Will I have to give up other things to say yes to this responsibility?

Remember that once you take on a responsibility, you should complete it. You can meet all of your responsibilities if you make careful choices along the way.

You have learned that you have a responsibility to yourself. You also have responsibilities to your friends, classmates, family, and community.

By acting responsibly you build your reputation. Each time you complete a responsibility, you prove that you can handle your duties.

Some of the responsibilities that you will take on will be larger and take longer to meet. Do not let a big responsibility scare you. Simply break it down into smaller parts. Make a plan that shows how the small jobs will add up to help you meet the big goal.

Suppose you decide to help your soccer team raise money for new uniforms. It is a big responsibility that you will not be able to finish in a weekend. With the help of

These bike riders pledged to raise at least $150 each for the National Multiple Sclerosis Society. They fulfilled their responsibilities by participating in the Escape to the Lake MS 150 Bike Tour in Jackson Township, Pennsylvania.

Sherman Avenue Elementary students Kiana Sanders, left, and Cameron Craft of Vicksburg, Mississippi, get sprayed while washing cars to raise money. The money is for victims of the September 11, 2001, terrorist attacks in New York and Washington, D.C.

your friends, however, you can plan a series of events. You might try a bake sale or a dog-washing service. Every event that you plan can also be divided into a series of steps. As you complete your step-by-step plan, you will be on your way to meeting your responsibility.

Your responsibilities do not stop with the people that you know. You are also a part of your community, your city, your state, and your country. You are part of the world. You can be a responsible citizen by finding answers for tough problems and helping others.

Glossary

Accountable: Accepting responsibility for your actions and their results

Commitment: A promise that you will stay with something

Conflict: A disagreement, argument, or source of tension

Obligation: Something that you have to do; duty

Perseverance: Sticking with a responsibility or task, no matter what; staying with a problem or challenge even when it is difficult

Reliability: Doing what you say you will do

Reputation: The positive or negative way that other people see you

Self-control: Staying in charge of your emotions and actions

Trustworthiness: The quality or state of deserving the confidence of others

Resources

Karnes, Frances A., and Suzanne M. Bean. *Girls and Young Women Leading the Way*. Minneapolis: Free Spirit Publishing, 1993.

This book includes 20 first-person accounts that will inspire boys and girls alike.

Krumgold, Joseph. *And Now Miguel*. New York: HarperTrophy, 1984.

A 12-year-old boy yearns for adult responsibilities, but does not foresee all the consequences of those responsibilities.

MacDonald, Margaret Read. *Peace Tales: World Folktales to Talk About*. North Haven, CT: Shoe String Press, Inc., 1992.

This collection of tales teaches that all people are responsible for peace.

www.peteducation.com

This web site offers information about responsible pet ownership.

Index